APPLE WATCH SERIES 10 USER GUIDE

Smart Solutions for Modern Living

MARCUS T. HOOKS

COPYRIGHT

TABLE OF CONTENTS

INTRODUCTION
Apple Watch Series 10 User Guide

The Apple Watch Series 10 is a revolutionary piece of technology that seamlessly combines innovation, style, and functionality. It is more than just a watch; it is a comprehensive smart device designed to enhance your daily life. From tracking your health to managing your time, the Apple Watch Series 10 offers unparalleled convenience, making it a must-have accessory for anyone looking to simplify and enrich their lifestyle. This guide will take you through every feature, function, and benefit of the Apple Watch Series 10, ensuring that you can harness its full potential.

A Decade of Evolution: The Journey to Series 10

The Apple Watch has come a long way since its debut. With every new series, Apple has refined its vision of what a smartwatch can be, integrating cutting-edge technology with user-focused design. The Series 10 marks a milestone—a culmination of ten years of innovation, offering features that redefine wearable technology. From its sleek design to its intuitive interface, the Series 10 represents Apple's commitment to pushing boundaries and enhancing user experiences.

In this chapter, we'll explore how the Apple Watch Series 10 stands apart from its predecessors. It combines advanced sensors, an upgraded processor, and a host of new features that cater to health enthusiasts, tech-savvy users, and professionals alike. By the end of this guide, you'll understand why the Apple Watch Series 10 is not just a gadget but an indispensable companion.

Unboxing the Apple Watch Series 10: First Impressions

Opening the box of your Apple Watch Series 10 is an experience in itself. Apple's meticulous packaging reflects the thoughtfulness of the product inside. Here's what you'll find in the box:

- The Apple Watch Series 10.

- A magnetic charging cable.

- Quick start guides and documentation.

- Optional bands, depending on your chosen model.

The first time you hold the watch, you'll notice its refined build and lightweight design. The Series 10 is available in a variety of finishes and sizes, ensuring there's a model that suits every preference. Whether you're upgrading from a previous version or purchasing an Apple Watch for the first time, the Series 10 sets a new standard for quality and elegance.

Why Choose the Apple Watch Series 10?

The Apple Watch Series 10 isn't just about keeping time; it's about saving time. With its enhanced capabilities, it empowers you to accomplish more with less effort. Here are some compelling reasons to choose this device:

- **Advanced Health Monitoring:** The Series 10 offers comprehensive health tracking, including ECG monitoring, blood oxygen measurement, and sleep tracking, allowing you to stay informed about your well-being.

- **Enhanced Performance:** Its next-generation processor ensures faster, smoother operation, making multitasking effortless.

- **Customizable Design:** With a variety of watch faces, bands, and complications, you can tailor your watch to reflect your personal style.

- **Seamless Integration:** The Series 10 works flawlessly with your iPhone and other Apple devices, creating a cohesive ecosystem that keeps you connected.

- **Durability and Longevity:** Designed with high-quality materials, the Apple Watch Series 10 is built to withstand daily wear and tear, offering years of reliable service.

The Future of Health and Fitness

One of the standout features of the Apple Watch Series 10 is its focus on health and fitness. The device goes beyond basic step counting, offering a suite of tools designed to help you achieve your wellness goals. With its advanced sensors, the Series 10 can track metrics such as:

- Heart rate variability.

- Blood oxygen levels.

- Sleep stages and quality.

- Calories burned during various activities.

For fitness enthusiasts, the watch offers guided workouts, personalized coaching, and even challenges to keep you motivated. The new watchOS update brings more workout types, including specialized options for activities like hiking, yoga, and swimming.

A Productivity Powerhouse on Your Wrist

The Apple Watch Series 10 isn't just for fitness fanatics. Its productivity features make it an invaluable tool for professionals and students. With Siri integration, you can set reminders, dictate notes, and even control smart home devices. The calendar and task management apps ensure you never miss a meeting or deadline.

Additionally, the Series 10 introduces a new multitasking interface, allowing you to switch between apps with ease. Notifications are more interactive, enabling you to reply to messages, accept calendar invites, or check your to-do list directly from your wrist. The Series 10 transforms your watch into a productivity hub, giving you the freedom to stay organized wherever you are.

Communication at Your Fingertips

Staying connected has never been easier. The Apple Watch Series 10 allows you to make calls, send texts, and even participate in video chats right from your wrist. With its improved microphone and speaker quality, conversations are clear and natural.

For those who prefer hands-free communication, the Series 10 supports Siri commands and voice-to-text functionality.

Whether you're sending a quick message or navigating a complex conversation, the Apple Watch ensures you remain accessible and efficient.

Innovation Meets Style

Apple has always been known for blending technology with aesthetics, and the Series 10 is no exception. The watch is available in a range of materials, including aluminum, stainless steel, and titanium. Each model is designed with precision, ensuring a balance between durability and elegance.

Customization is key with the Series 10. You can choose from a variety of watch faces, each offering unique complications that display real-time information. Whether you prefer a minimalist design or a data-rich interface, the Series 10 has options to suit your taste.

The Role of watchOS 10

The Apple Watch Series 10 runs on watchOS 10, the latest iteration of Apple's smartwatch operating system. This software update introduces several new features and optimizations, including:

- Redesigned app interfaces for easier navigation.

- Enhanced privacy controls for health data.

- Improved battery management for extended use.

- New gestures and shortcuts for quicker interactions.

watchOS 10 ensures that the hardware capabilities of the Series 10 are fully utilized, delivering a seamless and intuitive user experience.

Sustainability and Environmental Impact

Apple's commitment to sustainability is evident in the Series 10. The device is made with recycled materials, and its packaging is designed to minimize waste. Additionally, the watch's energy-efficient components help reduce its carbon footprint, making it an eco-friendly choice for tech enthusiasts.

By choosing the Apple Watch Series 10, you're not just investing in a powerful device; you're also supporting a company that values environmental responsibility.

Unlocking the Full Potential

The Apple Watch Series 10 is more than just a smartwatch; it's a transformative device that adapts to your lifestyle. Whether you're an athlete striving for peak performance, a professional managing a busy schedule, or someone who values staying connected, the Series 10 offers tools to meet your needs.

As you explore this user guide, you'll discover tips and tricks to optimize your experience. From setting up the device to mastering its advanced features, this guide is your comprehensive resource for getting the most out of your Apple Watch Series 10.

Welcome to the future of wearable technology. Let's get started!

CHAPTER 1

Overview of the Apple Watch Series 10

The Apple Watch Series 10 marks a significant leap forward in wearable technology, combining cutting-edge innovation with refined aesthetics. As the latest iteration in Apple's renowned smartwatch lineup, the Series 10 solidifies its position as a market leader by addressing consumer needs while introducing groundbreaking features. This device is more than just a timepiece—it's a powerful health companion, a productivity enhancer, and a stylish accessory.

Launched to much fanfare, the Series 10 builds upon its predecessors' strengths while offering enhancements that set it apart. The watch introduces an ultra-slim design with a larger and brighter Always-On Retina XDR display, delivering unparalleled clarity and responsiveness. Crafted from aerospace-grade titanium and durable ceramic, it balances elegance with durability. With its updated software, including watchOS 10, the device promises a seamless and intuitive user experience.

The Apple Watch Series 10 is engineered to cater to a wide array of lifestyles, from fitness enthusiasts and professionals to those seeking smarter ways to stay connected. It integrates seamlessly into Apple's ecosystem, making it an invaluable tool for anyone invested in the brand's products and services.

Key Features and Improvements Over Previous Models

The Apple Watch Series 10 introduces a host of advancements that elevate its functionality, comfort, and appeal. These improvements ensure it outpaces competitors and sets new benchmarks in wearable technology. Some key features and upgrades include:

1. **Enhanced Display Technology:** The Series 10 boasts an Always-On Retina XDR display that is 20% larger and 30% brighter than the Series 9. This improvement ensures superior visibility under all lighting conditions, whether you're outdoors in bright sunlight or indoors in dim settings. The edge-to-edge screen seamlessly blends into the watch's chassis, maximizing the display area without increasing the overall size.

2. **Advanced Processor:** Powered by the new S10 chip, the Apple Watch Series 10 delivers lightning-fast performance and energy efficiency. Tasks like opening apps, processing health data, and syncing with other devices are smoother than ever. The chip's Neural Engine also supports more complex on-

device machine learning tasks, enabling smarter and more personalized features.

3. **Revolutionary Health Features:** Building on Apple's commitment to health and wellness, the Series 10 introduces non-invasive glucose monitoring, enabling users to track their blood sugar levels effortlessly. The watch also improves its ECG capabilities, sleep tracking algorithms, and advanced menstrual cycle tracking, offering deeper insights into users' overall health.

4. **Satellite Connectivity:** For adventurers and outdoor enthusiasts, the Series 10 includes satellite connectivity. This feature allows users to send SOS messages or share their location even when outside cellular range, enhancing safety and peace of mind.

5. **Extended Battery Life:** Despite the more powerful hardware, the Series 10 provides up to 36 hours of battery life on a single charge. In power-saving mode, it can extend up to 72 hours, ensuring reliability for long trips or busy days.

6. **Improved Durability:** The Apple Watch Series 10 is built to withstand the elements. It is water-resistant up to 50 meters and now includes enhanced dust and

crack resistance, making it a durable companion for rigorous activities.

7. **Customized Bands and Colors:** Apple introduces an array of new bands and colors, catering to diverse tastes. From sustainable materials to luxurious leather options, users can express their personality while enjoying unmatched comfort.

8. **Enhanced watchOS 10:** The latest operating system brings redesigned widgets, improved navigation, and enhanced app functionality. Users can enjoy seamless integration with their iPhone, AirPods, and other Apple devices, unlocking a cohesive experience across the ecosystem.

Why the Apple Watch Series 10 is a Must-Have Device

The Apple Watch Series 10 is more than just a smartwatch; it's a lifestyle upgrade. Its innovative features and intuitive design make it an indispensable device for various aspects of daily life. Here's why the Series 10 stands out as a must-have:

1. **Unparalleled Health and Fitness Companion:** The Apple Watch Series 10's advanced health monitoring tools—including non-invasive glucose tracking,

blood oxygen monitoring, and improved sleep analysis—empower users to take control of their wellness. Fitness enthusiasts benefit from enhanced activity tracking, guided workouts, and metrics like VO2 Max and heart rate variability, making it an essential partner for achieving fitness goals.

2. **Seamless Connectivity:** Staying connected has never been easier. The Series 10 allows users to make calls, send texts, and receive notifications directly on their wrist. With satellite connectivity and improved cellular capabilities, it ensures users are reachable even in remote locations.

3. **Productivity On-the-Go:** With the Series 10, managing daily tasks is a breeze. From calendar reminders and email notifications to voice dictation and smart replies, the device keeps users organized and efficient. Its compatibility with third-party productivity apps further enhances its utility for professionals.

4. **Eco-Friendly Design:** Apple continues its commitment to sustainability with the Series 10. The device incorporates recycled materials and energy-efficient manufacturing processes, making it an

environmentally conscious choice without compromising performance.

5. **Stylish and Versatile:** Whether you're attending a business meeting or hitting the gym, the Series 10 adapts to any setting. Its sleek design, customizable watch faces, and interchangeable bands allow users to tailor the device to their preferences and occasions.

6. **Safety and Security:** Features like fall detection, emergency SOS, and satellite connectivity make the Series 10 a reliable safety tool. Parents, adventurers, and seniors alike can benefit from the watch's ability to provide assistance during emergencies.

7. **Investment in the Future:** The Apple Watch Series 10 exemplifies the future of wearable technology. By adopting this device, users gain access to cutting-edge features and ongoing software updates that will keep the device relevant and functional for years to come.

The Apple Watch Series 10 isn't just an accessory; it's a transformative device that enhances health, productivity, and connectivity. Its combination of innovation, design, and functionality ensures it remains the gold standard in the smartwatch industry, making it an irresistible choice for tech enthusiasts and casual users alike.

CHAPTER 2

Unboxing and Setup

What's in the Box?

The Apple Watch Series 10 arrives in a sleek and minimalist package that reflects Apple's commitment to design and sustainability. Opening the box is a seamless and satisfying experience, indicative of the premium product within. Here's what you can expect to find:

1. **Apple Watch Series 10**: The star of the show, your new watch, is securely nestled within a protective covering to ensure it arrives in pristine condition. Depending on your selection, the watch case material may be titanium, stainless steel, or aluminum, and the band will match your chosen style and size.

2. **Watch Band**: Apple includes the band selected during purchase, whether it's a sporty fluoroelastomer band, a stylish leather band, or a modern woven band. Many models also include an additional strap size to ensure the perfect fit.

3. **Magnetic Fast Charger to USB-C Cable**: The updated charging cable is designed to work

seamlessly with the Series 10, offering faster charging capabilities. The magnetic puck effortlessly snaps to the back of the watch, ensuring a secure connection every time.

4. **Quick Start Guide**: This concise booklet provides essential instructions for setting up your device, pairing it with your iPhone, and navigating the basic features. For more in-depth assistance, Apple encourages users to consult the Apple Support website or app.

5. **Regulatory Information and Warranty Documentation**: Standard paperwork outlining the product's warranty coverage and compliance with various regulatory standards is included.

Notably, Apple has eliminated the inclusion of a USB-C power adapter from the box to reduce environmental impact, a continuation of their commitment to sustainability. Users can use their existing adapter or purchase one separately if needed.

Charging the Apple Watch for the First Time

Before diving into the setup process, it's essential to charge your Apple Watch Series 10 to ensure optimal performance during initialization. Follow these steps to charge your watch:

1. **Unwrap the Watch and Charger**: Remove the protective coverings from your watch and charging cable.

2. **Connect the Charger**: Plug the USB-C end of the charging cable into a power adapter (not included) or a powered USB-C port on your computer. Place the magnetic charging puck on a flat surface.

3. **Attach the Watch**: Align the back of the Apple Watch with the magnetic puck. The magnets will guide the watch into place and hold it securely.

4. **Confirm Charging**: When correctly connected, the watch's screen will display a charging indicator. If the battery is completely drained, it may take a few moments before the screen lights up.

5. **Wait for Full Charge**: Allow the watch to charge until the battery reaches 100%, ensuring you start with maximum power. The Series 10's improved charging technology reduces charging times, so you'll be ready to go in about an hour for a full charge or even faster for a quick top-up.

Step-by-Step Setup Process and Pairing with Your Phone

The Apple Watch Series 10 is designed for an intuitive and straightforward setup. Below is a detailed guide to help you get your watch ready for use:

1. **Power On the Watch**: Press and hold the side button until the Apple logo appears on the screen. The watch will power on and guide you to the next steps.

2. **Select Your Language and Region**: Follow the on-screen prompts to choose your preferred language and region settings. These choices determine your device's interface and compatibility with local services.

3. **Bring Your iPhone Near**: Ensure your iPhone is running the latest version of iOS. Place it close to the Apple Watch, and a pairing screen should appear on your phone automatically. Tap "Continue." If the screen doesn't appear, open the Watch app on your iPhone and select "Pair a New Watch."

4. **Align the Watch with the Viewfinder**: Use your iPhone's camera to align the watch face with the on-screen viewfinder. This step pairs your devices securely. If alignment fails, you can choose manual

pairing by entering the code displayed on your Apple Watch into your phone.

5. **Restore from Backup or Set Up as New**: If you've previously owned an Apple Watch, you can restore your settings, apps, and preferences from a backup. If this is your first Apple Watch, choose "Set Up as New Watch."

6. **Sign in with Your Apple ID**: Enter your Apple ID credentials to unlock features like iCloud syncing, Apple Pay, and app downloads. Ensure two-factor authentication is enabled for added security.

7. **Configure Settings**: Follow the on-screen instructions to customize settings such as location services, Siri preferences, and Activity tracking. You can adjust these later in the Watch app.

8. **Sync Apps and Data**: Your Apple Watch will automatically sync apps and data from your iPhone that are compatible with watchOS 10. Depending on the volume of data, this process may take several minutes.

9. **Finish and Start Exploring**: Once setup is complete, you'll see the watch face on your Apple

Watch. Take a moment to familiarize yourself with basic navigation, such as using the Digital Crown and side button.

Customizing Your Watch Face

The Apple Watch Series 10 offers unparalleled customization options for its watch faces, allowing users to tailor the device to their style, mood, or needs. Follow these steps to personalize your watch face:

1. **Browse Available Watch Faces**: Press and hold the current watch face on your Apple Watch screen until the watch face menu appears. Swipe left or right to explore pre-installed faces. To add a new one, scroll to the end of the list and tap the "+" icon.

2. **Select a Watch Face**: Tap on the desired watch face to select it. Popular options include Modular, Infograph, and the newly introduced Solar Dial, each offering unique layouts and features.

3. **Customize Colors and Styles**: Once you've selected a face, tap "Edit" to adjust colors, styles, and complications. Use the Digital Crown to scroll through available options and find your preferred look.

4. **Add Complications**: Complications are small widgets that display useful information or provide quick access to apps. Examples include weather, calendar events, fitness metrics, and shortcuts to apps like Messages or Music. Select the complications you'd like to include, then position them on your watch face.

5. **Save Your Customization**: After finalizing your design, press the Digital Crown to save your customized watch face. It will now appear as your default face.

6. **Sync Across Devices**: If you'd like to manage watch faces from your iPhone, open the Watch app and navigate to the "Face Gallery" tab. Here, you can explore additional options, make edits, and sync changes to your Apple Watch.

7. **Switch Between Faces**: To quickly switch watch faces, press and hold the current face, then swipe left or right to choose another saved face. This flexibility allows you to adapt your watch's appearance and functionality throughout the day.

Unboxing and setting up your Apple Watch Series 10 is an exciting journey that highlights the device's seamless integration and intuitive design. From the elegantly packaged contents to the step-by-step pairing process and extensive customization options, every detail reflects Apple's dedication to user experience. With your watch fully charged, paired, and personalized, you're ready to explore its powerful features and elevate your daily life.

CHAPTER 3

Understanding the Interface

The Apple Watch Series 10 represents the pinnacle of intuitive design, merging hardware and software seamlessly to provide an unmatched user experience. Understanding the interface is key to harnessing the full power of this sophisticated device. This chapter delves into navigation basics, the home screen layout, and accessing key settings, empowering users to make the most of their Apple Watch.

Navigation Basics: Buttons, Digital Crown, and Touch Gestures

The navigation system on the Apple Watch Series 10 is designed for simplicity and efficiency, ensuring users can access features and information with minimal effort. Here's a comprehensive breakdown of the core navigation elements:

1. Buttons

- **Side Button:**

    o Located on the right side of the watch, the side button has several functions:

- Press once to access the Dock, which displays recently used apps and favorites.

- Double-press to activate Apple Pay for secure transactions.

- Press and hold to access the power menu, enabling options like Power Off, Medical ID, and Emergency SOS.

  o In some contexts, the side button serves as a secondary interaction mechanism, such as confirming actions.

- **Digital Crown:**

  o Positioned above the side button, the Digital Crown is a versatile tool that enhances navigation:

    - Rotate to scroll through content, adjust settings, or zoom in and out on maps and photos.

    - Press once to return to the watch face or access the home screen.

- Press and hold to activate Siri for voice commands.

- Double-press to switch between the last used apps.

2. Touch Gestures

The touch-sensitive display of the Apple Watch offers intuitive gestures for navigating the interface:

- **Tap:**

  o Use a single tap to select apps, buttons, or menu items.

- **Swipe:**

  o Swipe left or right to navigate between pages within apps.

  o Swipe up from the bottom of the watch face to access the Control Center.

  o Swipe down from the top of the watch face to view notifications.

- **Force Touch (Legacy):**

  o Although deprecated in recent watchOS versions, older users may be familiar with pressing firmly on the screen to reveal contextual menus. Instead, watchOS 10 now incorporates these actions into the interface.

- **Touch and Hold:**

  o   Touch and hold the watch face to enter the customization mode for changing watch faces.

3. Voice Interaction

Siri, Apple's voice assistant, adds a hands-free dimension to navigation:

- Activate Siri by saying "Hey Siri," pressing and holding the Digital Crown, or raising your wrist and speaking directly.

- Use Siri for tasks like setting reminders, sending messages, or opening apps.

Overview of the Home Screen and App Layout

The home screen of the Apple Watch Series 10 is the central hub for accessing apps and features. Its design prioritizes usability and aesthetic appeal, making it easy for users to find and open apps.

1. Grid View vs. List View

Users can choose between two layouts for the home screen:

- **Grid View:**

    o Displays apps as a honeycomb-like arrangement of circular icons.

    o Navigate by swiping and zooming using the Digital Crown.

    o Tap an icon to open the corresponding app.

    o Apps are automatically arranged, but you can reposition icons by touching and holding them until they jiggle, then dragging them to a new location.

- **List View:**

    o Shows apps in an alphabetized list for easy navigation.

    o Scroll through the list using the Digital Crown or swipe gestures.

    o Switch between views by pressing and holding the home screen and selecting your preferred option.

2. Organizing Apps

- Use the Watch app on your iPhone to reorganize apps and create a layout that suits your preferences.

- Delete unwanted apps directly on the watch by touching and holding an app icon (in Grid View) and tapping the "X" button or swiping left in List View.

3. App Dock

The Dock provides quick access to your most-used apps:

- Press the side button to open the Dock.

- Customize the Dock to show recent apps or a curated list of favorites by adjusting settings in the Watch app.

- Swipe left or right to switch between apps.

4. Watch Faces as a Launch Point

- Watch faces aren't just for displaying time; they act as functional launch points for complications, which provide quick access to app data or shortcuts.

- For example, tapping the weather complication opens the Weather app, while tapping the activity rings opens the Fitness app.

Key Settings and How to Access Them

The Apple Watch's settings allow users to fine-tune their experience, from display preferences to privacy controls. Here's how to navigate and utilize these settings effectively:

1. Accessing Settings

- Open the **Settings app** directly on your watch by tapping its icon on the home screen.

- Alternatively, use the Watch app on your iPhone for a more comprehensive view and easier navigation.

2. Display and Brightness

- Adjust brightness levels to suit your environment by navigating to **Settings > Display & Brightness**.

- Enable or disable the **Always-On Display** to balance convenience and battery life.

- Modify text size and enable bold text for improved readability.

3. Notifications

- Manage app notifications to avoid unnecessary distractions:

o Go to **Settings** > **Notifications** to toggle alerts for individual apps.

o Customize notification styles to ensure important alerts are prominent while others are minimized.

4. Connectivity

- Set up and manage Wi-Fi and Bluetooth connections under **Settings** > **Wi-Fi** and **Settings** > **Bluetooth**.

- Pair accessories like AirPods for seamless audio playback.

- Check cellular connectivity and data usage if your watch supports LTE.

5. Privacy and Security

- Protect your Apple Watch with a passcode. Enable this in **Settings** > **Passcode**.

- Use **Unlock with iPhone** to simplify unlocking your watch when nearby.

- Manage privacy settings for health data, location tracking, and Siri interactions under **Settings** > **Privacy**.

6. Health and Fitness Settings

- Customize activity goals and metrics under **Settings > Activity**.

- Enable features like fall detection, heart rate monitoring, and emergency SOS in **Settings > Health**.

- Sync workout data with the Fitness app on your iPhone for detailed insights.

7. System and Software

- Update watchOS by navigating to **Settings > General > Software Update** or through the Watch app on your iPhone.

- Restart or reset your watch if needed by going to **Settings > General > Restart** or **Reset**.

8. Accessibility Options

- Enable features like VoiceOver, Zoom, and Assistive Touch in **Settings > Accessibility**.

- Adjust these settings to enhance usability for individuals with specific needs.

Mastering the interface of the Apple Watch Series 10 is the key to unlocking its full potential. With its intuitive navigation system, versatile home screen layout, and customizable settings, the watch adapts effortlessly to your needs. By understanding these elements, users can enjoy a seamless, efficient, and personalized experience that enhances both productivity and convenience.

CHAPTER 4

Health and Fitness Features

The Apple Watch Series 10 redefines health and fitness tracking with its state-of-the-art sensors, enhanced algorithms, and intuitive features. Designed to empower users to take charge of their well-being, this chapter explores the watch's ability to monitor workouts, track vital health metrics, and leverage its new health sensors and alerts.

Tracking Workouts and Activities

The Apple Watch Series 10 is a versatile fitness companion, catering to users of all activity levels. Its advanced tracking features ensure accuracy and comprehensiveness, helping users achieve their fitness goals.

1. Comprehensive Workout Tracking

The **Workout app** is at the heart of fitness tracking on the Apple Watch:

- **Choosing a Workout Type:**

  - The app offers a variety of workout types, including running, cycling, swimming, yoga, HIIT, and strength training. For those with unique routines, the "Other" category ensures no activity goes untracked.

- **Real-Time Metrics:**

  o During a workout, the watch displays essential metrics such as heart rate, calories burned, distance, and duration. Use the Digital Crown to toggle between screens for additional data like elevation and cadence.

- **Customizable Goals:**

  o Set goals for calories, distance, or time. The watch provides real-time feedback, motivating you to stay on track.

2. Automatic Workout Detection

- The Apple Watch Series 10 can detect common activities like walking, running, or cycling automatically. If you forget to start a workout manually, the watch prompts you to log it and retroactively records your activity.

3. Activity Rings

The Activity Rings provide a holistic view of your daily movement:

- **Move Ring:** Tracks active calories burned throughout the day. Set personalized goals based on your lifestyle.

- **Exercise Ring:** Encourages at least 30 minutes of moderate activity daily. Any workout that raises your heart rate contributes to closing this ring.

- **Stand Ring:** Promotes regular movement by reminding you to stand and stretch once an hour.

4. Fitness Challenges and Awards

- Participate in monthly challenges or compete with friends to close rings and achieve personal bests. Awards and badges provide additional motivation.

5. Third-Party Fitness Apps

- Sync with apps like Strava, Nike Training Club, and Peloton for a more tailored fitness experience. These apps seamlessly integrate with Apple's Activity app, providing detailed insights and unique challenges.

Monitoring Heart Rate, Sleep, and Blood Oxygen Levels

The Apple Watch Series 10's health monitoring capabilities go beyond fitness, offering tools to track vital metrics and provide actionable insights into your overall well-being.

1. Heart Rate Monitoring

The watch's advanced heart rate sensor is integral to its health tracking:

- **Resting and Active Heart Rate:**
    - Measure your resting heart rate to gauge fitness levels or track your heart rate during workouts to optimize performance.

- **High and Low Heart Rate Alerts:**
    - The watch sends notifications if your heart rate exceeds or falls below preset thresholds, helping you identify potential health issues early.

- **ECG App:**
    - Take an electrocardiogram to detect irregular heart rhythms like atrial fibrillation. The ECG app records a waveform that can be shared with your doctor for further analysis.

2. Sleep Tracking

Sleep tracking on the Apple Watch Series 10 offers a detailed understanding of your sleep patterns:

- **Sleep Stages:**

  - The Sleep app categorizes your rest into REM, Core, and Deep stages, providing insights into the quality of your sleep.

- **Bedtime Routine:**

  - Set a bedtime schedule with wind-down reminders to establish a consistent sleep pattern.

- **Trends Over Time:**

  - Track sleep duration and quality trends in the Health app on your iPhone to identify improvements or issues.

3. Blood Oxygen Monitoring

The blood oxygen sensor is a game-changer for health monitoring:

- **SpO2 Readings:**

  - Measure blood oxygen levels on demand or enable periodic readings throughout the day and night.

- **Health Implications:**

  - Low SpO2 levels can indicate respiratory or circulatory issues. Monitoring this metric is especially useful for individuals with chronic conditions or high-altitude enthusiasts.

- **Integration with Fitness:**

  - Use blood oxygen data to gauge recovery and performance after intense workouts.

Using the New Health Sensors and Alerts

The Apple Watch Series 10 introduces cutting-edge health sensors that expand its capabilities, making it a powerful tool for proactive health management.

1. Non-Invasive Glucose Monitoring

- **Revolutionary Technology:**

  - The Series 10 features non-invasive glucose monitoring, allowing users to track blood sugar levels without pricking their skin. This feature benefits diabetics and those monitoring dietary impacts on blood sugar.

- **Real-Time Alerts:**

  - Receive notifications if glucose levels deviate from normal ranges, helping you take immediate corrective actions.

2. Temperature Sensor

- **Menstrual Cycle Tracking:**

  - The temperature sensor enhances the accuracy of ovulation and menstrual cycle tracking, providing valuable insights for family planning or understanding hormonal health.

- **Illness Detection:**

  - Slight changes in body temperature can signal the onset of illness, allowing users to seek early medical intervention.

3. Fall Detection and Emergency SOS

- **Advanced Fall Detection:**

  - The Series 10's improved accelerometer and gyroscope detect hard falls. If a fall is detected, the watch prompts you to confirm your safety. If you don't respond, it automatically contacts emergency services and shares your location.

- **Emergency SOS:**

  o Press and hold the side button to activate Emergency SOS. This feature notifies local authorities and your emergency contacts.

4. Atrial Fibrillation History

- **Long-Term Monitoring:**

  o The watch now tracks atrial fibrillation (AFib) over time, offering insights into frequency and patterns. This data is invaluable for individuals managing chronic heart conditions.

5. Respiratory Rate Monitoring

- **Sleep and Stress Insights:**

  o Measure your respiratory rate while sleeping to detect signs of sleep apnea or other respiratory issues.

- **Mindfulness Integration:**

  o Combine respiratory rate data with the Mindfulness app for stress management and relaxation techniques.

6. Real-Time Alerts and Trends

- **Customizable Alerts:**

  o Set thresholds for metrics like heart rate, blood oxygen, and respiratory rate. The watch provides real-time notifications if values deviate from your set range.

- **Trend Analysis:**

  o Use the Health app to analyze trends over weeks or months, helping you identify patterns and make informed decisions about your lifestyle.

The Apple Watch Series 10's health and fitness features represent a paradigm shift in wearable technology. With its advanced tracking capabilities, comprehensive health monitoring, and groundbreaking sensors, the watch serves as a personal health assistant, fitness coach, and safety device. By leveraging these features, users can take a proactive approach to their health and well-being, making the Series 10 an indispensable tool in today's fast-paced world.

CHAPTER 5

Communication and Connectivity

The apple Watch Series 10 is more than just a smartwatch—it's a communication hub that keeps you connected with the world in ways that are efficient, seamless, and versatile. From making calls and sending messages to utilizing the Walkie-Talkie feature and connecting with Wi-Fi, Bluetooth, and cellular networks, the Series 10 ensures you're always within reach. This chapter explores these capabilities in detail, highlighting how the apple Watch transforms everyday communication.

Making Calls and Sending Messages

One of the standout features of the apple Watch Series 10 is its ability to make calls and send messages directly from your wrist. Whether you're out for a run, in a meeting, or simply don't have your phone handy, the watch ensures that communication is always just a tap away.

1. Making Calls

The Japple Watch Series 10 allows you to make calls using:

- **Cellular Connectivity** (if your model supports it):

- With a cellular-enabled watch, you can make and receive calls without needing your phone nearby. This is ideal for activities like jogging or running errands.

- **Bluetooth Connection to Your Phone**:

  - When paired with your phone, the watch routes calls through the phone's network, allowing you to answer directly from the watch.

- **Siri Voice Commands**:

  - Simply say, "Hey Siri, call [contact's name]," and the watch will place the call for you.

How to Make a Call

1. Press the side button or tap the Phone app on your watch.

2. Browse recent calls or use the Digital Crown to scroll through your contacts.

3. Tap the desired contact or dial the number manually using the keypad.

4. Press the green call button to initiate the call.

2. Sending Messages

The Messages app on the apple Watch Series 10 is optimized for quick and convenient texting. You can compose messages in multiple ways:

- **Dictation**:
    - Speak your message, and the watch will transcribe it into text.

- **Quick Replies**:
    - Choose from a list of preset responses that you can customize via the Watch app on your phone.

- **Scribble**:
    - Use your finger to draw letters on the screen, and the watch converts them into text.

- **Emoji and GIFs**:
    - Add personality to your messages with emojis and animated stickers.

How to Send a Message

1. Open the Messages app on your watch.

2. Select a conversation or tap "New Message."

3. Choose the recipient from your contacts or enter their number.

4. Compose your message using dictation, scribble, or a quick reply.

5. Tap the send button to deliver your message.

The ability to make calls and send messages directly from your wrist ensures that you can stay connected even in situations where pulling out your phone isn't practical.

Using the Walkie-Talkie Feature

The Walkie-Talkie feature on the apple Watch Series 10 is a unique and fun way to communicate in real time. It's perfect for quick exchanges, coordinating plans, or staying in touch with friends and family during activities.

1. Setting Up Walkie-Talkie

Before you can use the Walkie-Talkie feature, ensure that:

- Both you and the person you wish to communicate with have Walkie-Talkie enabled.

- You've accepted the initial invitation to connect via the Walkie-Talkie app.

To set up:

1. Open the Walkie-Talkie app on your watch.

2. Tap "Add Friends" and select a contact.

3. Wait for them to accept your invitation.

2. Using Walkie-Talkie

1. Open the Walkie-Talkie app and select a contact.

2. Press and hold the Talk button to speak. Your message will play instantly on their watch.

3. Release the button when you're finished. The other person can respond by pressing their Talk button.

3. Key Features of Walkie-Talkie

- **Real-Time Communication**:
  - Messages are transmitted instantly, replicating the experience of using a traditional walkie-talkie.

- **Voice Notifications**:
  - If the recipient isn't actively using their watch, they'll receive a voice notification prompting them to join the conversation.

- **Privacy Controls**:

  - You can toggle your availability on and off, ensuring you're not interrupted when you need focus time.

The Walkie-Talkie feature is an innovative addition to the apple Watch Series 10, combining convenience and spontaneity for on-the-go communication.

Connecting with Wi-Fi, Bluetooth, and Cellular Networks

Seamless connectivity is at the core of the apple Watch Series 10's functionality. Whether you're syncing with your phone, accessing the internet, or relying on cellular data, the watch offers robust connectivity options.

1. Wi-Fi Connectivity

The apple Watch Series 10 automatically connects to known Wi-Fi networks when your phone isn't nearby. This ensures continued access to features like:

- Sending and receiving messages.

- Using Siri.

- Accessing apps that require an internet connection.

How to Connect to Wi-Fi:

1. Open the Settings app on your watch.

2. Tap "Wi-Fi" and select a network from the list.

3. Enter the password if required.

4. The watch will remember this network for future use.

2. Bluetooth Connectivity

Bluetooth is essential for pairing your watch with your phone and other devices, such as wireless headphones. The Japple Watch Series 10 uses Bluetooth 5.0 for faster and more reliable connections.

How to Pair Devices via Bluetooth:

1. Put your Bluetooth device in pairing mode.

2. Open the Settings app on your watch and tap "Bluetooth."

3. Select the device from the list and wait for the connection to establish

3. Cellular Connectivity

Cellular-enabled models of the apple Watch Series 10 provide unmatched independence from your phone. With an active cellular plan, you can:

- Make calls and send messages.

- Stream music and podcasts.

- Access navigation and location services.

How to Set Up Cellular:

1. Open the Watch app on your phone.

2. Navigate to "Cellular" and follow the on-screen instructions to activate a plan.

3. Ensure your carrier supports apple Watch cellular plans.

Key Features of Cellular Connectivity:

- **Emergency SOS**: Contact emergency services even if your phone isn't nearby.

- **Family Setup**: Configure a watch for a family member without them needing their own phone.

Tips for Optimizing Connectivity

1. **Switch Between Wi-Fi and Cellular Efficiently**:

   o Enable Wi-Fi Assist to prioritize stronger connections.

2. **Update Network Settings Regularly**:

   o Ensure your watch's firmware is up to date for optimal performance.

3. **Monitor Battery Usage**:

   o Cellular connectivity consumes more power. Use Wi-Fi or Bluetooth when possible to conserve battery life.

4. **Troubleshoot Connectivity Issues**:

   o Restart your watch and phone or reset network settings if you encounter problems.

The apple Watch Series 10's communication and connectivity features make it a powerful tool for staying connected in today's fast-paced world. Whether you're making calls, sending messages, using the Walkie-Talkie feature, or leveraging Wi-Fi, Bluetooth, and cellular networks, the watch ensures you're always in touch. By mastering these capabilities, you'll unlock the full potential of your device, making it an indispensable part of your daily life.

CHAPTER 6

Productivity and Smart Tools

Calendar, Reminders, and Notes on Your Watch

The Apple Watch Series 10 is designed to enhance your productivity by bringing powerful organizational tools directly to your wrist. With seamless integration into Apple's ecosystem, apps like Calendar, Reminders, and Notes ensure that you stay on top of your schedule and tasks without needing to reach for your phone.

Calendar on Apple Watch

Your Apple Watch allows you to access and manage your calendar effortlessly. Here's how it keeps you organized:

1. **Viewing Your Schedule:** The Calendar app displays a clear and concise overview of your day, week, or month. Use the Digital Crown to scroll through events or tap an event to view its details. You can also switch between views for a more detailed perspective.

2. **Receiving Event Notifications:** Notifications for upcoming events appear on your watch, ensuring you're always aware of what's next. Alerts can be

customized to notify you minutes, hours, or even a day in advance.

3. **Adding Events:** While the watch does not support typing for creating new events, you can use Siri to add events quickly. Simply say, "Add an event to my calendar for [date and time]," and Siri will handle the rest.

4. **Syncing Across Devices:** Any changes made on your Apple Watch sync instantly with your iPhone, iPad, and Mac via iCloud. This ensures your schedule is up-to-date no matter which device you use.

Reminders on Apple Watch

The Reminders app on Apple Watch is a powerful tool for managing tasks and to-do lists. With its intuitive interface and voice command capabilities, it makes staying organized easier than ever.

1. **Creating Reminders:** Use Siri to add reminders by saying, "Remind me to [task] at [time]." You can also tap the "+ New Reminder" option in the app to create one manually.

2. **Categorizing Tasks:** Organize your reminders into lists, such as "Work," "Groceries," or "Personal," to

keep things tidy. You can switch between lists directly on your watch.

3. **Time and Location Alerts:** Reminders can be set to trigger based on time or location. For example, you can create a reminder to "Pick up milk" when you arrive at the grocery store.

4. **Completing Tasks:** Mark tasks as complete with a simple tap. The app's interface makes it easy to track your progress.

Notes on Apple Watch

While the Notes app on the Apple Watch is more limited than on larger devices, it still provides key functionalities that are useful for productivity:

1. **Viewing Notes:** Use the third-party app integration or Notes widget to view important notes synced from your iPhone or iCloud.

2. **Dictating New Notes:** With Siri, you can dictate quick notes by saying, "Take a note," followed by the content you want to save.

3. **Syncing Across Devices:** Notes created on your watch will sync automatically with your other Apple

devices, ensuring consistency across your ecosystem.

Using Siri and Voice Commands Effectively

Siri, Apple's virtual assistant, plays a vital role in making the Apple Watch Series 10 a truly hands-free productivity tool. With advanced voice recognition and natural language processing, Siri helps you perform tasks, get information, and control devices effortlessly.

Activating Siri

1. **Using "Hey Siri":** Simply say, "Hey Siri," followed by your request. This hands-free method is ideal for situations where your hands are occupied.

2. **Raising Your Wrist:** Raise your wrist and speak directly to the Apple Watch to activate Siri without saying the wake phrase.

3. **Pressing the Digital Crown:** Press and hold the Digital Crown to manually activate Siri, ensuring it's ready to take your command.

Productivity with Siri

1. **Setting Timers and Alarms:** Siri can quickly set timers and alarms, making it easier to stay on track.

For example, say, "Set a timer for 15 minutes" or "Wake me up at 7 a.m."

2. **Managing Your Schedule:** Use Siri to add events to your calendar, create reminders, and check your daily agenda. Siri can also provide information about upcoming meetings and appointments.

3. **Sending Messages and Emails:** Dictate messages and emails directly from your watch. Siri can send texts, read received messages aloud, and even respond to emails when synced with your iPhone.

4. **Searching for Information:** Ask Siri to find information online, such as weather updates, news, or trivia. For instance, "What's the weather like today?" or "What's the latest stock price for Apple?"

5. **Navigating with Maps:** Siri can guide you to a location by setting directions in the Maps app. Say, "Get directions to [destination]," and your watch will provide turn-by-turn navigation.

6. **Controlling Music and Media:** Use Siri to play, pause, skip tracks, or adjust the volume for music and other media. For example, say, "Play my workout playlist."

Tips for Effective Siri Use

- Speak clearly and naturally for better recognition.

- Use specific and concise commands.

- Ensure your watch is connected to Wi-Fi or cellular for optimal performance.

Integration with Smart Home Devices

The Apple Watch Series 10 serves as a convenient hub for managing your smart home ecosystem. Through the Home app and Siri, you can control a wide range of devices, enhancing convenience and automation.

Using the Home App

1. **Accessing Smart Devices:** The Home app on your Apple Watch allows you to control compatible smart home devices, such as lights, thermostats, cameras, and locks. Devices must be connected to your HomeKit network.

2. **Monitoring Your Home:** View real-time updates from security cameras, check sensor readings, or see if doors and windows are locked—all directly from your wrist.

3. **Creating Scenes:** Automate multiple actions with a single command by creating scenes. For instance, a "Good Night" scene can turn off lights, lock doors, and adjust the thermostat.

4. **Receiving Notifications:** The watch provides alerts for motion detection, doorbell activity, and other events, keeping you informed no matter where you are.

Using Siri for Smart Home Control

Siri simplifies smart home management by allowing you to control devices with voice commands. Examples include:

- "Turn on the living room lights."

- "Set the thermostat to 72 degrees."

- "Lock the front door."

- "Start the coffee maker."

Advanced Smart Home Integration

1. **Automation Routines:** Use the Home app to create automation routines based on time, location, or device triggers. For example, set the lights to turn on when you arrive home or the blinds to close at sunset.

2. **Third-Party Integrations:** Many third-party devices are compatible with HomeKit, expanding the range of devices you can control. From smart speakers to air purifiers, your Apple Watch can manage a wide array of gadgets.

3. **Remote Access:** With an Apple Home Hub (e.g., HomePod or Apple TV), you can control your smart home devices remotely, even when you're away from home.

The Apple Watch Series 10 is a productivity powerhouse, equipped with tools to keep you organized, efficient, and connected. Whether managing your schedule, leveraging Siri for hands-free commands, or controlling your smart home, this device simplifies your daily life in meaningful ways. Its seamless integration with Apple's ecosystem and smart home technology ensures that everything you need is always just a glance or command away, making it an indispensable tool for modern living.

CHAPTER 7

Entertainment and Apps

Listening to Music, Podcasts, and Audiobooks

The Apple Watch Series 10 is not just a productivity powerhouse; it's also a versatile entertainment device. Whether you're a music enthusiast, a podcast addict, or an audiobook lover, the watch offers seamless access to your favorite content directly from your wrist.

Music on Apple Watch

The Apple Watch makes it easy to enjoy music anytime, anywhere. Here's how:

1. **Apple Music Integration:** If you're an Apple Music subscriber, you can stream songs directly to your watch when connected to Wi-Fi or cellular. With over 90 million songs available, you'll always have access to your favorite artists and playlists.

2. **Offline Listening:** For times when you're away from your phone or Wi-Fi, you can download songs and playlists directly to your Apple Watch. Open the Apple Music app, find your desired playlist or album, and select "Download to Watch."

3. **Controlling Playback:** Use the Digital Crown to adjust volume and swipe on the screen to skip tracks or pause playback. Voice commands like "Hey Siri, play [song/artist]" make navigation even easier.

4. **Third-Party Music Apps:** Spotify, Pandora, and other popular music apps are compatible with the Apple Watch. They offer features like offline playback and curated playlists, extending your music experience.

Podcasts on Apple Watch

Podcasts are a fantastic way to stay informed and entertained, and the Apple Watch Series 10 makes it simple to dive into your favorite shows:

1. **Apple Podcasts App:** The native Podcasts app syncs with your iPhone, allowing you to pick up where you left off. Episodes can be streamed or downloaded directly to the watch for offline listening.

2. **Discover New Podcasts:** Browse trending or recommended episodes using the app's intuitive interface. Siri can also assist by finding shows based on your interests.

3. **Third-Party Apps:** Apps like Overcast and Pocket Casts provide additional features, such as custom playlists and enhanced playback controls, further enhancing your podcast experience.

Audiobooks on Apple Watch

Transform your downtime into an immersive storytelling experience with audiobooks:

1. **Apple Books Integration:** Purchase and download audiobooks on your iPhone, then sync them to your Apple Watch. The Books app provides a straightforward interface for browsing and playback.

2. **Listening Made Easy:** Use the Digital Crown to navigate chapters and adjust playback speed directly on your watch. Siri commands like "Play my audiobook" offer hands-free convenience.

3. **Third-Party Audiobook Apps:** Audible, Libby, and other popular apps allow you to access an extensive library of audiobooks. Many of these apps support offline playback and personalized recommendations.

Exploring Third-Party Apps and Installing Them

The Apple Watch Series 10's app ecosystem is robust, with thousands of third-party apps designed to expand its functionality. From productivity tools to fitness trackers and creative utilities, the App Store offers something for everyone.

Finding and Installing Apps

1. **Accessing the App Store:** Open the App Store app on your Apple Watch to browse and download apps directly. The intuitive interface categorizes apps by type, such as "Health & Fitness," "Productivity," and "Games."

2. **Using Your iPhone:** Alternatively, use the Watch app on your iPhone to search for and install apps. This method provides a larger screen and easier navigation.

3. **Syncing Apps Automatically:** Enable the "Automatic App Install" option in the Watch app settings. This feature ensures that compatible apps downloaded on your iPhone are automatically installed on your Apple Watch.

4. **Managing Installed Apps:** To organize your apps, press and hold an app icon on the watch's home screen until the icons jiggle. Drag them to rearrange or tap the "X" to uninstall unwanted apps.

Must-Have Third-Party Apps

1. **Fitness and Health:** Apps like Strava, MyFitnessPal, and WaterMinder provide enhanced fitness tracking and goal setting.

2. **Travel and Navigation:** Use Citymapper for detailed public transport directions or iTranslate for instant language translations on the go.

3. **Productivity:** Todoist and Evernote help you stay organized and manage tasks efficiently.

4. **Creative Tools:** Apps like Procreate Pocket and Canva offer creative outlets directly on your wrist.

5. **Finance:** Monitor your finances with apps like Mint and Robinhood, which provide updates on budgets and stock performance.

Customizing App Settings

Personalize app permissions and notifications to suit your preferences. Navigate to the Watch app on your iPhone, select an app, and adjust settings such as location access, background refresh, and notification preferences.

Playing Games and Other Entertainment Options

While gaming may not be the first thing that comes to mind for a smartwatch, the Apple Watch Series 10 offers a surprisingly fun and engaging gaming experience. With its advanced hardware and optimized apps, it caters to casual gamers and entertainment seekers alike.

Gaming on Apple Watch

1. **Puzzle Games:** Games like "Tiny Armies" and "Rules!" offer quick, brain-teasing challenges that are perfect for the small screen.

2. **Trivia and Word Games:** Enjoy classics like "Trivia Crack" or "Wordie" to test your knowledge and vocabulary.

3. **Action and Arcade Games:** While limited by screen size, games like "Bubblegum Hero" and "Lifeline" provide simple but addictive gameplay.

4. **Fitness-Based Games:** Combine gaming with exercise using apps like "Zombies, Run!" that

gamify your workouts and encourage physical activity.

Other Entertainment Options

1. **Streaming Services:** Use apps like Apple TV and YouTube Music to control playback and explore content directly from your watch.

2. **Photo Viewing:** Sync albums from your iPhone to your Apple Watch and enjoy a miniature slideshow of your favorite memories.

3. **Social Media:** Apps like Instagram and Twitter provide lightweight versions for quick browsing and updates.

4. **Mindfulness and Relaxation:** Apps like Calm and Breathe offer guided meditations and relaxation exercises, turning your watch into a tool for mental wellness.

The Apple Watch Series 10 redefines entertainment and app functionality in the wearable space. Its integration with music, podcasts, and audiobooks ensures you're always entertained, while access to thousands of third-party apps expands its capabilities beyond imagination. With gaming options and other innovative features, the Series 10 proves it's more than just a productivity tool—it's a device that brings joy, creativity, and relaxation to your everyday life.

CHAPTER 8

Customization and Style

Changing Watch Bands and Cases

One of the standout features of the Apple Watch Series 10 is its unparalleled customization, allowing users to adapt their device to suit any occasion, outfit, or personal style. From changing watch bands to selecting cases that reflect your personality, the Apple Watch offers endless possibilities.

Changing Watch Bands

Apple has designed the watch bands to be easily interchangeable, enabling users to switch between styles without hassle. Here's how to change your watch band and explore the variety of options available:

1. **Removing the Current Band:**

   o Turn the watch face down on a soft surface to avoid scratches.

   o Locate the band release buttons on the back of the case. Press and hold the button while sliding the band to the side to remove it.

2. **Attaching a New Band:**

   o Align the new band with the grooves on the watch case.

   o Slide it into place until you hear a soft click, indicating that the band is securely attached.

3. **Choosing the Right Band:**

   o **Sport Bands:** Made from durable fluoroelastomer, these bands are ideal for workouts and casual settings.

   o **Leather Bands:** Perfect for formal occasions, leather bands offer a touch of elegance and sophistication.

   o **Milanese Loop:** This stainless-steel mesh band combines style and comfort, making it a versatile choice for any setting.

   o **Woven Nylon and Solo Loops:** These bands prioritize comfort and are available in a variety of vibrant colors.

4. **Caring for Your Bands:**

   o Clean sport bands with a damp cloth and mild soap.

o Use a dry, non-abrasive cloth for leather bands and avoid excessive exposure to moisture.

Customizing the Watch Case

While the watch case isn't interchangeable, selecting the right case material and finish during purchase ensures a device that reflects your taste. The Apple Watch Series 10 offers:

1. **Aluminum Cases:** Lightweight and available in several colors, these are perfect for everyday wear.

2. **Stainless Steel Cases:** Durable and polished, they provide a luxurious look suitable for formal occasions.

3. **Titanium Cases:** Combining strength and elegance, titanium is ideal for users who prioritize durability.

4. **Ceramic Cases:** A premium option known for its sleek, glossy finish and high durability.

Personalizing Watch Faces and Complications

One of the most exciting aspects of the Apple Watch is the ability to personalize your watch face, tailoring it to your needs and style. The Series 10 takes this customization further with a vast array of watch faces and advanced complications.

Choosing and Customizing Watch Faces

1. **Selecting a Watch Face:**

   o Press and hold the current watch face until the customization menu appears.

   o Swipe left or right to browse through available faces or tap the "+" icon to add a new one.

2. **Editing the Design:**

   o Tap "Edit" to access customization options.

   o Adjust the color, style, and layout using the Digital Crown.

   o Choose faces that reflect your lifestyle, such as the "Modular" face for productivity or "Chronograph" for a classic look.

3. **New Faces in watchOS 10:**

   o The Series 10 introduces exclusive watch faces, such as dynamic solar patterns and animated visualizations for fitness metrics.

Adding and Managing Complications

Complications are small widgets that display critical information or provide quick access to apps. Adding the right complications can enhance your watch's functionality.

1. **Popular Complications:**

   - **Activity Rings:** Track your movement, exercise, and standing goals.

   - **Weather:** Stay informed about temperature, precipitation, and UV index.

   - **Calendar:** View your next event at a glance.

   - **Battery Life:** Monitor your watch's remaining charge.

2. **Customizing Complications:**

   - Open the Watch app on your iPhone and select the "My Faces" tab.

   - Tap a watch face, then choose complications to add or rearrange.

3. **Using Third-Party Complications:**

   o Install apps like CARROT Weather or Strava to access unique complications tailored to specific tasks or interests.

4. **Switching Between Faces:**

   o Save multiple faces for different occasions. Swipe left or right on the watch face screen to switch between them effortlessly.

Advanced Settings for a Tailored Experience

The Apple Watch Series 10's advanced settings allow users to fine-tune their device for a truly personalized experience. These settings cover everything from display preferences to accessibility features.

Display and Brightness

1. **Always-On Display:**

   o Enable the Always-On Retina XDR display to keep your watch face visible at all times, even when your wrist is down.

   o Adjust brightness levels in the Settings app to optimize visibility and battery life.

2. **Text Size and Bold Text:**

   o Customize text size for readability. Open the Settings app, go to "Display & Brightness," and adjust the text size slider.

   o Toggle "Bold Text" for improved clarity.

Haptics and Sounds

1. **Haptic Feedback:**

   o Enable or adjust haptic feedback for a tactile response when receiving notifications or interacting with the watch.

   o Access this setting under "Sounds & Haptics" in the Settings app.

2. **Silent Mode:**

   o Activate Silent Mode to mute sounds while retaining haptic alerts. Swipe up on the watch face to access the Control Center and tap the bell icon.

Health and Fitness Settings

1. **Heart Rate Monitoring:**

    o Enable continuous heart rate tracking in the Health app for detailed insights.

    o Set high and low heart rate alerts to stay informed about irregular patterns.

2. **Workout Preferences:**

    o Customize metrics displayed during workouts, such as pace, distance, and calories burned.

    o Enable Auto-Pause for activities like running or cycling, ensuring accuracy when you take breaks.

Accessibility Features

The Apple Watch Series 10 offers comprehensive accessibility settings to cater to diverse needs:

1. **VoiceOver:**

    o Activate VoiceOver to hear spoken descriptions of on-screen elements. Navigate to "Accessibility" in the Settings app to enable this feature.

2. **Zoom:**

   o Use the Zoom function to magnify elements on the screen for better visibility. Adjust the zoom level with the Digital Crown.

3. **AssistiveTouch:**

   o Enable AssistiveTouch to control the watch using hand gestures, perfect for users with limited mobility.

Notifications and Focus Modes

1. **Managing Notifications:**

   o Customize notification settings to ensure you only receive alerts that matter. Navigate to "Notifications" in the Watch app on your iPhone to adjust preferences.

2. **Focus Modes:**

   o Sync Focus settings with your iPhone to minimize distractions during work, exercise, or relaxation.

Customizing Control Center and Dock

1. **Control Center:**

    o   Rearrange Control Center icons for quick
        access to frequently used settings. Swipe up
        on the watch face, tap "Edit," and drag icons
        to rearrange.

2. **Dock Preferences:**

    o   Choose between "Recents" and "Favorites"
        to organize the Dock. Access this setting via
        the Watch app on your iPhone.

The Apple Watch Series 10's extensive customization
options make it a device like no other. Whether you're
swapping bands for a new look, personalizing your watch
face with complications, or fine-tuning advanced settings,
the Series 10 empowers you to create a device that aligns
perfectly with your lifestyle and preferences. Its adaptability
ensures that it's not just a smartwatch but a true extension of
your personality.

CHAPTER 9

Troubleshooting and Maintenance

Common Issues and How to Fix Them

The Apple Watch Series 10 is engineered for reliability and performance, but like any advanced piece of technology, users may encounter occasional issues. Understanding common problems and their solutions can help ensure your device runs smoothly.

1. Connectivity Issues

Problem: The Apple Watch fails to connect to your iPhone or Wi-Fi.

Solution:

- **Check Bluetooth and Wi-Fi**: Ensure both Bluetooth and Wi-Fi are enabled on your iPhone and Apple Watch.

- **Restart Both Devices**: Restart your Apple Watch and iPhone to refresh their connections.

- **Forget and Re-Pair**: Open the Watch app on your iPhone, unpair the watch, and then pair it again.

- **Update Software**: Make sure both devices are running the latest versions of iOS and watchOS.

2. Battery Draining Quickly

Problem: The battery life is shorter than expected.

Solution:

- **Check Background Apps**: Close unused apps running in the background by pressing the side button and swiping up on apps in the Dock.

- **Disable Always-On Display**: Turn off the Always-On Display in the Settings app to save power.

- **Adjust Notifications**: Limit unnecessary notifications through the Watch app on your iPhone.

- **Enable Power Saving Mode**: Use Low Power Mode for extended battery life.

3. Watch Not Charging

Problem: The Apple Watch does not charge when connected to the magnetic charger.

Solution:

- **Clean the Charger and Watch Back**: Dust and debris can interfere with charging. Use a soft, lint-free cloth to clean the surfaces.

- **Try Another Outlet or Adapter**: Test the charger with a different power outlet or adapter.

- **Restart the Watch**: A quick restart may resolve the issue.

- **Inspect for Damage**: Check the charger and cable for signs of wear or damage.

4. Frozen or Unresponsive Watch

Problem: The Apple Watch screen freezes or becomes unresponsive.

Solution:

- **Force Restart**: Press and hold both the side button and Digital Crown for at least 10 seconds until the Apple logo appears.

- **Close Problematic Apps**: Identify and close any apps that may be causing the issue.

- **Reset to Factory Settings**: As a last resort, erase all content and settings via the Watch app on your iPhone, then set up the watch as new.

5. Inaccurate Health Data

Problem: Heart rate, step count, or other health metrics appear incorrect.

Solution:

- **Adjust Fit**: Ensure the watch is snug but comfortable on your wrist.

- **Recalibrate Activity Tracking**: Go to the Watch app, select "Privacy," and choose "Reset Fitness Calibration Data."

- **Update watchOS**: Bugs affecting sensors may be fixed in software updates.

Software Updates and Backups

Keeping your Apple Watch Series 10 updated and backed up ensures optimal performance and security. Here's how to manage these processes:

Updating watchOS

1. **Prepare Your Devices**:

    o Ensure your iPhone is updated to the latest version of iOS.

- Place the Apple Watch on its charger and ensure it has at least 50% battery life.

- Connect your iPhone to Wi-Fi.

2. **Update via iPhone**:

- Open the Watch app on your iPhone.

- Navigate to "General" > "Software Update."

- If an update is available, tap "Download and Install." Follow on-screen instructions.

3. **Update Directly on the Watch**:

- Open "Settings" on your Apple Watch.

- Go to "General" > "Software Update."

- If an update is available, tap "Download and Install." Ensure the watch remains on its charger during the update.

Backing Up Your Apple Watch

Apple Watch backups occur automatically when paired with an iPhone. Here's how to ensure your data is safe:

1. **Automatic Backups**:

   o When the Apple Watch is unpaired from your iPhone, a backup is created automatically.

   o These backups are included in your iPhone's iCloud or iTunes backup.

2. **Manual Unpairing to Trigger Backup**:

   o Open the Watch app on your iPhone.

   o Select your watch and tap "Unpair Apple Watch." This process creates a backup.

3. **Restoring from Backup**:

   o When setting up a new Apple Watch, you'll be prompted to restore from a backup. Select the desired backup to transfer your settings and data.

Cleaning and Caring for Your Watch

Proper maintenance extends the life of your Apple Watch and ensures it remains functional and attractive. Here's how to clean and care for your device:

Cleaning the Watch Case and Display

1. **Materials Needed**:

   o Use a soft, lint-free cloth.

   o For stubborn smudges, slightly dampen the cloth with fresh water.

2. **Cleaning Steps**:

   o Power off the watch and remove it from the charger.

   o Wipe the case and display gently with the cloth.

   o Avoid using abrasive materials, soaps, or cleaning agents.

3. **Special Care for Materials**:

   o For stainless steel and titanium cases, polish gently to maintain their shine.

   o Ceramic cases should be cleaned with water and a microfiber cloth for a streak-free finish.

Maintaining the Watch Band

1. **Sport Bands**:

   o Wash with water and mild soap.

   o Dry with a soft cloth before reattaching.

2. **Leather Bands**:

   o Avoid water exposure.

   o Clean with a dry, soft cloth and store in a cool, dry place when not in use.

3. **Metal Bands**:

   o Use a damp cloth for cleaning.

   o Dry thoroughly to prevent rust or tarnishing.

Protecting Your Apple Watch

1. **Use a Screen Protector**:

   o Apply a screen protector to prevent scratches and cracks.

2. **Avoid Extreme Conditions**:

   o Keep the watch away from extreme temperatures, direct sunlight, and humid environments.

3. **Store Properly**:

   o When not in use, store the watch in a protective case or on a clean, dry surface.

Water Resistance Maintenance

The Apple Watch Series 10 is water-resistant but not waterproof. To maintain its water-resistance:

1. **Rinse After Exposure**:

   o After swimming or sweating, rinse the watch under fresh water and dry it thoroughly.

2. **Avoid Certain Liquids**:

   o Keep the watch away from soaps, shampoos, and perfumes, which can degrade seals.

3. **Check Water Ejection**:

   o Use the Water Lock feature to eject any trapped water from the speaker. Turn the Digital Crown to activate it.

Maintaining and troubleshooting your Apple Watch Series 10 doesn't have to be complicated. By addressing common issues promptly, keeping the software updated, and caring for your device properly, you ensure it remains a reliable companion for years to come. Whether it's cleaning the watch, optimizing settings, or backing up data, these practices keep your Apple Watch functioning at its best.

CHAPTER 10
Advanced Tips and Tricks

Hidden Features and Shortcuts

The Apple Watch Series 10 is packed with features that go beyond the obvious, offering shortcuts and hidden capabilities that can transform how you use your device. These advanced tips can help you unlock its full potential.

1. Quick Access Shortcuts

- **Control Center Customization:** Access the Control Center by swiping up from the bottom of the watch face. Tap "Edit" to rearrange icons or add shortcuts for features like Silent Mode, Theater Mode, and Water Lock.

- **Double-Tap to Switch Apps:** Press the side button twice to quickly switch between your most recently used apps.

- **Take a Screenshot:** Capture a screenshot by pressing the Digital Crown and the side button simultaneously. Make sure this feature is enabled in the Watch app on your iPhone.

- **Find Your iPhone:** Swipe up to open the Control Center and tap the phone icon to ping your iPhone. If it's dark, tap and hold the icon to activate the iPhone's flashlight.

2. Advanced Features

- **Handwashing Timer:** Enable the Handwashing Timer in the Watch app to ensure you're washing your hands for the recommended 20 seconds. The watch uses motion sensors and sound recognition to detect handwashing.

- **Track Sleep with Precision:** Use the enhanced Sleep app to monitor your sleep stages, including REM, Core, and Deep sleep. Set sleep goals and track trends over time.

- **Unlock Your Mac:** Automatically unlock your Mac when wearing your Apple Watch. Enable this feature in the Security & Privacy settings on your Mac.

- **Walkie-Talkie Mode:** Use the Walkie-Talkie app to send quick voice messages to other Apple Watch users. It's a fun and efficient way to stay connected.

- **Accessibility Gestures:** With AssistiveTouch, control your Apple Watch using gestures like clenching your fist or pinching your fingers. This feature is especially helpful for users with limited mobility.

Maximizing Battery Life

The Apple Watch Series 10 offers improved battery life, but with advanced features, usage patterns can significantly impact performance. These strategies can help you make the most of your battery:

1. Optimize Settings

- **Adjust Screen Brightness:** Lower the brightness in the Settings app under "Display & Brightness" to conserve energy.

- **Turn Off Always-On Display:** If battery life is a concern, disable the Always-On Display to extend usage.

- **Limit Background App Refresh:** In the Watch app, go to "General" > "Background App Refresh" and disable it for non-essential apps.

- **Use Power Saving Mode During Workouts:** Enable Power Saving Mode during workouts to disable the heart rate sensor and conserve battery.

2. Manage Notifications

- **Customize Notifications:** Reduce interruptions by limiting notifications to essential apps. Manage this in the Watch app on your iPhone under "Notifications."

- **Use Focus Modes:** Sync Focus settings from your iPhone to reduce notifications during specific activities, such as workouts or meetings.

3. Charge Smartly

- **Fast Charging:** The Series 10 supports rapid charging. Use the supplied USB-C cable and a compatible adapter to quickly top up your battery.

- **Battery Health Management:** Enable "Optimized Battery Charging" in the Settings app to reduce battery aging. This feature slows charging past 80% when the watch predicts prolonged use.

4. Monitor Usage

- **Check Battery Usage:** In the Watch app, navigate to "Battery" to view which apps and features consume the most energy. Adjust your usage accordingly.

- **Regularly Update Software:** Apple frequently releases updates to improve battery efficiency. Keep your watchOS up to date.

Exploring New Integrations with Other Apple Devices

The Apple Watch Series 10 seamlessly integrates with Apple's ecosystem, enhancing its functionality and delivering a cohesive experience across devices. Here's how to make the most of these integrations:

1. Seamless Interaction with iPhone

- **Camera Remote:** Use your Apple Watch to control your iPhone's camera. Open the Camera app on your watch to preview shots, set timers, or capture photos remotely.

- **Apple Pay:** Sync your credit or debit cards in the Wallet app on your iPhone to make secure payments directly from your wrist.

- **Handoff Feature:** Start tasks on your Apple Watch and continue them on your iPhone. For example, open an email on your watch and finish composing it on your phone.

2. Enhanced Experience with AirPods

- **Automatic Switching:** AirPods seamlessly switch between your Apple devices, including the watch. Start listening to music on your iPhone and switch to a workout playlist on your watch effortlessly.

- **Spatial Audio Control:** Use your watch to adjust Spatial Audio settings when using AirPods Pro or AirPods Max.

3. Integration with Mac

- **Continuity Features:** Use your Apple Watch to unlock your Mac, approve app installations, or access sensitive settings without entering a password.

- **Music and Media Control:** Control media playback on your Mac directly from your watch. This is especially useful during presentations or when your Mac is connected to an external display.

4. Apple TV Compatibility

- **Remote Control:** Turn your Apple Watch into a remote for your Apple TV. Navigate menus, play content, and adjust volume with ease.

- **Fitness+ Integration:** Sync your workouts to Apple TV for a more immersive experience. View metrics like heart rate and calories burned on the big screen.

5. Smart Home Integration with HomeKit

- **Control Devices:** Use the Home app on your Apple Watch to manage HomeKit-enabled devices. Turn on lights, adjust the thermostat, or lock doors directly from your wrist.

- **Scenes and Automations:** Activate pre-set scenes like "Good Night" or "Movie Time" with a tap or a voice command using Siri.

6. Fitness and Health Ecosystem

- **Health App Synchronization:** Data from your Apple Watch's sensors syncs with the Health app on your iPhone, providing a comprehensive view of your fitness and wellness trends.

- **Third-Party Fitness Apps:** Use apps like Peloton or Nike Run Club to integrate workouts seamlessly into your fitness routine.

7. Enhanced Productivity Tools

- **Notes and Reminders:** Create and manage notes or reminders on your Apple Watch, and sync them instantly with your iPhone, iPad, or Mac.

- **Calendar Synchronization:** Schedule events and receive reminders across all your Apple devices. The watch provides timely notifications, ensuring you never miss an appointment.

The Apple Watch Series 10 is more than a smartwatch; it's a gateway to advanced capabilities that enhance productivity, entertainment, and connectivity. By mastering hidden features, optimizing battery performance, and leveraging its integration with other Apple devices, you can unlock the full potential of your Apple Watch. Whether you're a tech enthusiast or a casual user, these advanced tips and tricks ensure a seamless and enriched experience, making your watch an indispensable part of your daily life.

CONCLUSION
Apple Watch Series 10 User Guide

The Apple Watch Series 10 is more than just a smartwatch; it is an embodiment of innovation, design excellence, and functionality. From its cutting-edge health monitoring features to its seamless integration within the Apple ecosystem, the Series 10 exemplifies what a modern wearable device can achieve. This guide has explored its myriad features, delving into the ways it enhances productivity, entertainment, connectivity, and personalization. As we wrap up this comprehensive journey through the Series 10's capabilities, it's clear that this device is not just a tool but a lifestyle companion that adapts to the unique needs of every user.

A Revolution in Health and Fitness

The Series 10 sets a new standard for health and fitness tracking. With its advanced sensors, it provides users with real-time insights into their physical well-being. The ability to monitor heart rate, blood oxygen levels, sleep patterns, and temperature variations ensures that you are always informed about your health status.

Fitness enthusiasts can benefit immensely from its workout tracking capabilities. The Activity Rings offer a simple yet effective way to stay motivated, while the extensive workout modes cater to every type of exercise. Whether you're running, swimming, or practicing yoga, the Series 10 helps you measure and achieve your fitness goals.

Beyond physical fitness, the watch's stress management tools and mindfulness features promote mental well-being, making it an all-encompassing health companion. It's not just about tracking data; it's about empowering users to lead healthier, more balanced lives.

Seamless Communication and Connectivity

The Series 10 redefines how we stay connected in today's fast-paced world. Its ability to make calls, send messages, and receive notifications directly from your wrist ensures you're always within reach, even when your phone is out of sight. Features like the Walkie-Talkie function and Siri make communication more dynamic and engaging.

With its robust connectivity options, including Wi-Fi, Bluetooth, and cellular capabilities, the Series 10 ensures you're never disconnected. Whether you're on a hike or navigating a busy day in the city, this watch keeps you linked to the people and information that matter most.

Productivity and Smart Tools

The Apple Watch Series 10 is a productivity powerhouse. Its suite of tools, including the calendar, reminders, and notes, helps users manage their schedules efficiently. The integration of Siri and voice commands adds a layer of convenience, allowing you to set reminders, check your calendar, or dictate notes hands-free.

The watch also excels in its smart home integration, turning it into a control center for your environment. From adjusting the thermostat to locking doors, the Series 10 simplifies and enhances daily living.

Entertainment at Your Fingertips

Entertainment is another area where the Series 10 shines. With the ability to stream music, podcasts, and audiobooks, the watch ensures you always have access to your favorite content. The addition of third-party apps and casual games further expands its entertainment potential, making it a versatile companion for work and play.

Personalization and Style

One of the Series 10's most appealing aspects is its adaptability to personal style. With interchangeable bands, customizable watch faces, and advanced settings, users can create a device that reflects their personality and lifestyle. Whether you're dressing for a formal event or gearing up for a workout, the Series 10 adapts to suit the occasion.

Advanced Features and Integrations

The Series 10's advanced features, such as hidden shortcuts and integrations with other Apple devices, make it a cornerstone of the Apple ecosystem. Its ability to unlock Macs, control AirPods, and interact with HomeKit devices highlights its role as a central hub for all things Apple. These integrations not only enhance convenience but also create a seamless, interconnected digital experience.

Reliability Through Troubleshooting and Maintenance

Maintaining the Apple Watch Series 10 is straightforward, thanks to its user-friendly design and durable build. Troubleshooting common issues, updating software, and cleaning the device regularly ensure it continues to function at its best. With proper care, the Series 10 is built to last, making it a worthwhile investment for years to come.

Looking Ahead: The Future of Wearable Technology

The Apple Watch Series 10 is not just a culmination of Apple's achievements in wearable technology; it's a glimpse into the future. With continuous updates and innovations, the

Series 10 lays the groundwork for even more advanced capabilities in the years to come. As health tracking becomes more sophisticated and smart home integration evolves, the potential for wearable devices like the Series 10 is limitless.

Why the Series 10 Is a Must-Have Device

The Apple Watch Series 10 is more than a gadget; it's a companion that enhances every aspect of your life. Its versatility, performance, and seamless integration into daily routines make it a must-have for anyone looking to improve their health, productivity, and connectivity. Whether you're an athlete, a professional, or someone who values convenience, the Series 10 has something to offer.

Final Thoughts

The journey through the Apple Watch Series 10's capabilities reveals a device that is both innovative and practical. Its ability to adapt to individual needs, coupled with its sleek design and powerful features, makes it a standout in the world of wearable technology. By mastering the tips, tricks, and functionalities outlined in this guide, you can unlock the full potential of your Series 10, transforming it into an indispensable part of your daily life.

Thank you for exploring the Apple Watch Series 10 User Guide. Whether you're a long-time Apple enthusiast or a first-time user, we hope this guide has equipped you with the knowledge to make the most of your watch. Here's to a future of enhanced living with the Apple Watch Series 10.